# THREE-MINUTE
## *Encores*

### 18 UNEXPECTED POP ETUDES FOR THE CONCERT STAGE

Arranged by Phillip Keveren

— PIANO LEVEL —
INTERMEDIATE TO ADVANCED

ISBN 978-1-70513-710-9

HAL•LEONARD®

For all works contained herein:
Unauthorized copying, arranging, adapting, recording, internet posting, public performance,
or other distribution of the music in this publication is an infringement of copyright.
Infringers are liable under the law.

Visit Hal Leonard Online at
**www.halleonard.com**

Visit Phillip at
**www.phillipkeveren.com**

Contact us:
**Hal Leonard**
7777 West Bluemound Road
Milwaukee, WI 53213
Email: info@halleonard.com

In Europe, contact:
**Hal Leonard Europe Limited**
42 Wigmore Street
Marylebone, London, W1U 2RN
Email: info@halleonardeurope.com

In Australia, contact:
**Hal Leonard Australia Pty. Ltd.**
4 Lentara Court
Cheltenham, Victoria, 3192 Australia
Email: info@halleonard.com.au

# PREFACE

## en·core

*noun*

**a repeated or additional performance of an item at the end of a concert, as called for by an audience.**

As the last note hangs in the air, there is a magical moment when an audience will – once in a while – decide they want to hear more! Not a lot more, mind you. The clock is ticking and the babysitter can only stay until 10 pm. But, can we make this evening last just a little longer?

The songs in this collection were arranged to serve as effective encores in a piano recital. Chosen from the popular music world, each selection is most likely known by many – if not most – of the people in the audience. Some are meant to be fun, colorful sparklers; others are poignant parting statements. Performance time of under three minutes will "leave them wanting more!"

Break a leg!

*Phillip Keveren*

# BIOGRAPHY

Phillip Keveren, a multi-talented keyboard artist and composer, has composed original works in a variety of genres from piano solo to symphonic orchestra. He gives frequent concerts and workshops for teachers and their students in the United States, Canada, Europe, and Asia. Mr. Keveren holds a B.M. in composition from California State University Northridge and a M.M. in composition from the University of Southern California.

# CONTENTS

# ALL THE THINGS YOU ARE

## from VERY WARM FOR MAY

Lyrics by OSCAR HAMMERSTEIN II
Music by JEROME KERN
Arranged by Phillip Keveren

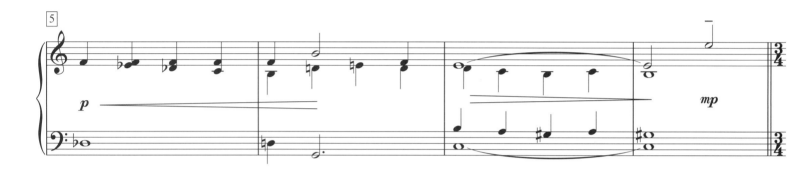

Copyright © 1939 UNIVERSAL - POLYGRAM INTERNATIONAL PUBLISHING, INC.
Copyright Renewed
This arrangement Copyright © 2022 UNIVERSAL - POLYGRAM INTERNATIONAL PUBLISHING, INC.
All Rights Reserved   Used by Permission

# BE OUR GUEST

## from BEAUTY AND THE BEAST

Lyrics by HOWARD ASHMAN
Music by ALAN MENKEN
Arranged by Phillip Keveren

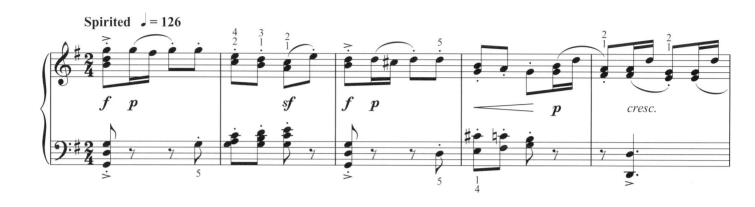

© 1991 Wonderland Music Company, Inc. and Walt Disney Music Company
This arrangement Copyright © 2012 Wonderland Music Company, Inc. and Walt Disney Music Company
All Rights Reserved.  Used by Permission.

# CRAZY LITTLE THING CALLED LOVE

Words and Music by
FREDDIE MERCURY
Arranged by Phillip Keveren

Copyright © 1979 Queen Music Ltd.
This arrangement Copyright © 2016 Queen Music Ltd.
All Rights Administered by Sony Music Publishing LLC, 424 Church Street, Suite 1200, Nashville, TN 37219
International Copyright Secured    All Rights Reserved

# CAN'T HELP FALLING IN LOVE
## from the Paramount Picture BLUE HAWAII

Words and Music by GEORGE DAVID WEISS,
HUGO PERETTI and LUIGI CREATORE
Arranged by Phillip Keveren

Freely expressive ♩ = c. 72

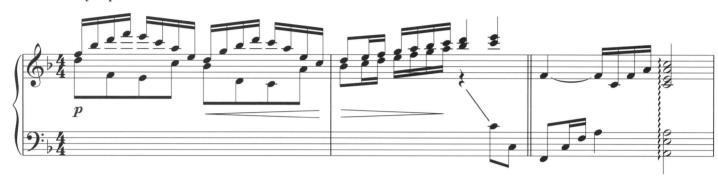

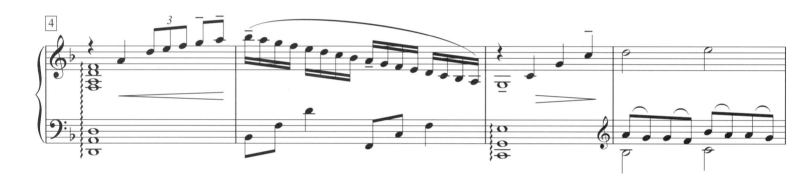

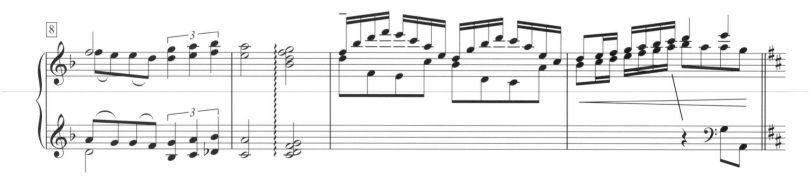

Copyright © 1961 Gladys Music
Copyright Renewed
Extended U.S. Renewal and British Reversionary Territories Assigned to Abilene Music LLC, HJP Music, Hugo Peretti Music and Luigi Creatore Music
This arrangement Copyright © 2022 Abilene Music LLC, HJP Music, Hugo Peretti Music and Luigi Creatore Music
Administered in the United States during the Extended Renewal by Steve Peter Music
All Rights Reserved   Used by Permission

# DANCING QUEEN

Words and Music by BENNY ANDERSSON,
BJÖRN ULVAEUS and STIG ANDERSON
Arranged by Phillip Keveren

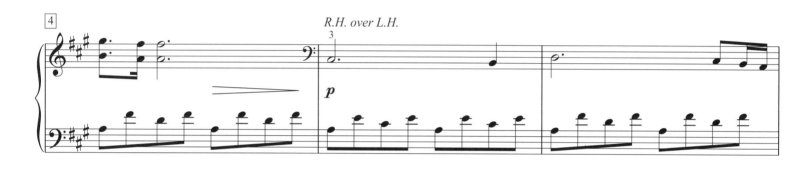

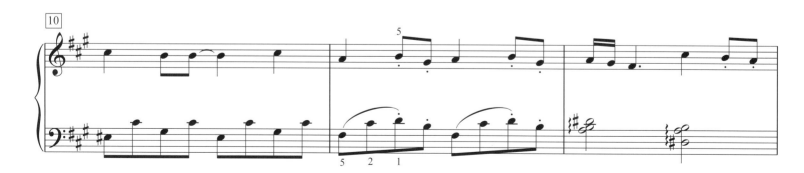

Copyright © 1976, 1977 UNIVERSAL/UNION SONGS MUSIKFORLAG AB
Copyright Renewed
This arrangement Copyright © 2016 UNIVERSAL/UNION SONGS MUSIKFORLAG AB
All Rights Administered by UNIVERSAL - POLYGRAM INTERNATIONAL PUBLISHING, INC. and EMI GROVE PARK MUSIC, INC.
All Rights Reserved   Used by Permission

# GOOD VIBRATIONS

Words and Music by BRIAN WILSON
and MIKE LOVE
Arranged by Phillip Keveren

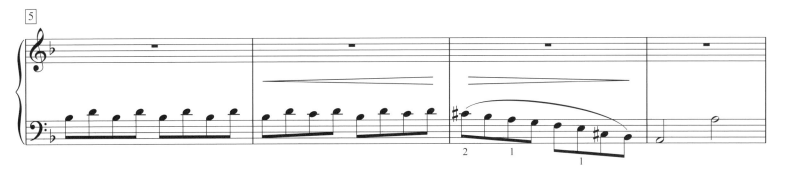

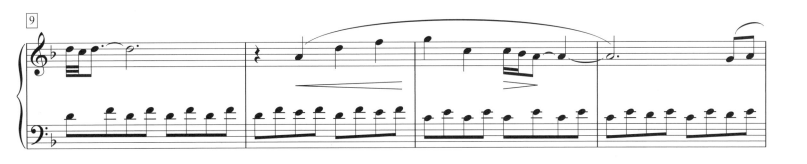

Copyright © 1966 IRVING MUSIC, INC.
Copyright Renewed
This arrangement Copyright © 2022 IRVING MUSIC, INC.
All Rights Reserved    Used by Permission

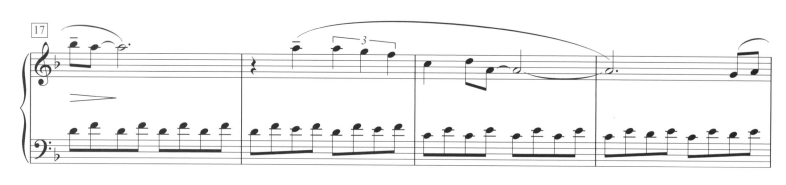

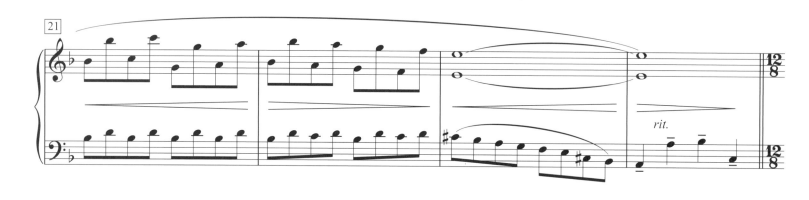

# GOODBYE TO LOVE

Words and Music by RICHARD CARPENTER
and JOHN BETTIS
Arranged by Phillip Keveren

Copyright © 1972 HAMMER AND NAILS MUSIC and ALMO MUSIC CORP.
Copyright Renewed
This arrangement Copyright © 2022 HAMMER AND NAILS MUSIC and ALMO MUSIC CORP.
All Rights Administered by ALMO MUSIC CORP.
All Rights Reserved   Used by Permission

# THE GREATEST SHOW

## from THE GREATEST SHOWMAN

Words and Music by BENJ PASEK,
JUSTIN PAUL and RYAN LEWIS
Arranged by Phillip Keveren

Copyright © 2017 Breathelike Music, Pick In A Pinch Music, T C F Music Publishing, Inc., Warner-Tamerlane Publishing Corp. and Spokane Boy Music
This arrangement Copyright © 2022 Breathelike Music, Pick In A Pinch Music, T C F Music Publishing, Inc., Warner-Tamerlane Publishing Corp. and Spokane Boy Music
All Rights for Breathelike Music and Pick In A Pinch Music Administered Worldwide by Kobalt Songs Music Publishing
All Rights for Spokane Boy Music Administered by Warner-Tamerlane Publishing Corp.
All Rights Reserved   Used by Permission

# HAVANA

Words and Music by CAMILA CABELLO,
LOUIS BELL, PHARRELL WILLIAMS,
ADAM FEENEY, ALI TAMPOSI,
JEFFERY LAMAR WILLIAMS, BRIAN LEE,
ANDREW WOTMAN, BRITTANY HAZZARD
and KAAN GUNESBERK
Arranged by Phillip Keveren

**With drama** ♩ = 108

Copyright © 2017 Maidmetal Limited, Milamoon Songs, Sony Music Publishing (UK), EMI April Music Inc., EMI Pop Music Publishing, More Water From Nazareth, EMI Blackwood Music Inc.,
EMI Music Publishing Ltd., Nyankingmusic, Sam Fam Beats, Reservoir 416, Young Stoner Life Publishing LLC, Andrew Watt Music, These Are Songs Of Pulse,
People Over Planes, Warner-Tamerlane Publishing Corp., Songs From The Dong, Atlantic Songs, 300 Rainwater Music and Universal Music Corp.
This arrangement Copyright © 2022 Maidmetal Limited, Milamoon Songs, Sony Music Publishing (UK), EMI April Music Inc., EMI Pop Music Publishing, More Water From Nazareth,
EMI Blackwood Music Inc., EMI Music Publishing Ltd., Nyankingmusic, Sam Fam Beats, Reservoir 416, Young Stoner Life Publishing LLC, Andrew Watt Music, These Are Songs Of Pulse,
People Over Planes, Warner-Tamerlane Publishing Corp., Songs From The Dong and Atlantic Songs, 300 Rainwater Music and Universal Music Corp.
All Rights on behalf of Maidmetal Limited, Milamoon Songs, Sony Music Publishing (UK), EMI April Music Inc., EMI Pop Music Publishing, More Water From Nazareth, EMI Blackwood Music Inc.,
EMI Music Publishing Ltd., Nyankingmusic and Sam Fam Beats Administered by Sony Music Publishing LLC, 424 Church Street, Suite 1200, Nashville, TN 37219
All Rights on behalf of Reservoir 416 and Young Stoner Life Publishing LLC Administered Worldwide by Reservoir Media Management, Inc.
All Rights on behalf of Andrew Watt Music Administered Worldwide by Songs Of Kobalt Music Publishing
All Rights on behalf of These are Songs Of Pulse and People Over Planes Administered by Concord Sounds c/o Concord Music Publishing
All Rights on behalf of Songs From The Dong and Atlantic Songs Administered by Warner-Tamerlane Publishing Corp.
All Rights on behalf of 300 Rainwater Music Administered by Songs Of Universal, Inc.
International Copyright Secured   All Rights Reserved

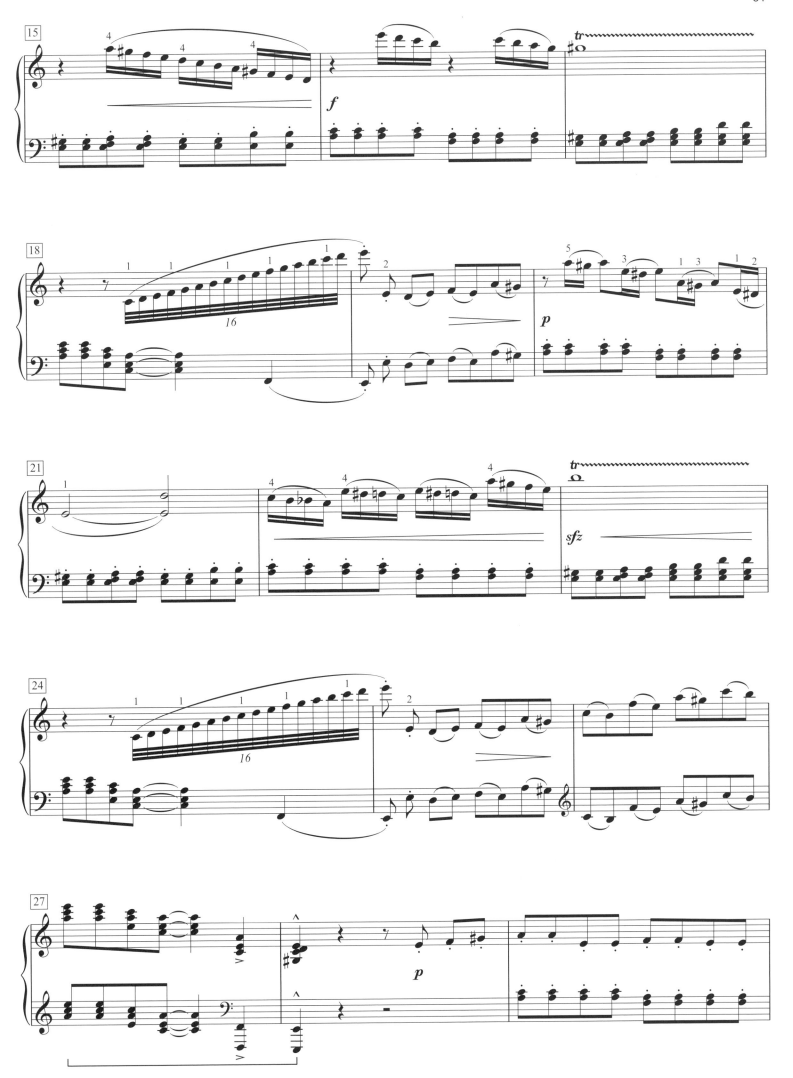

# HEY JUDE

Words and Music by JOHN LENNON
and PAUL McCARTNEY
Arranged by Phillip Keveren

Copyright © 1968 Sony Music Publishing LLC
Copyright Renewed
This arrangement Copyright © 2022 Sony Music Publishing LLC
All Rights Administered by Sony Music Publishing LLC, 424 Church Street, Suite 1200, Nashville, TN 37219
International Copyright Secured   All Rights Reserved

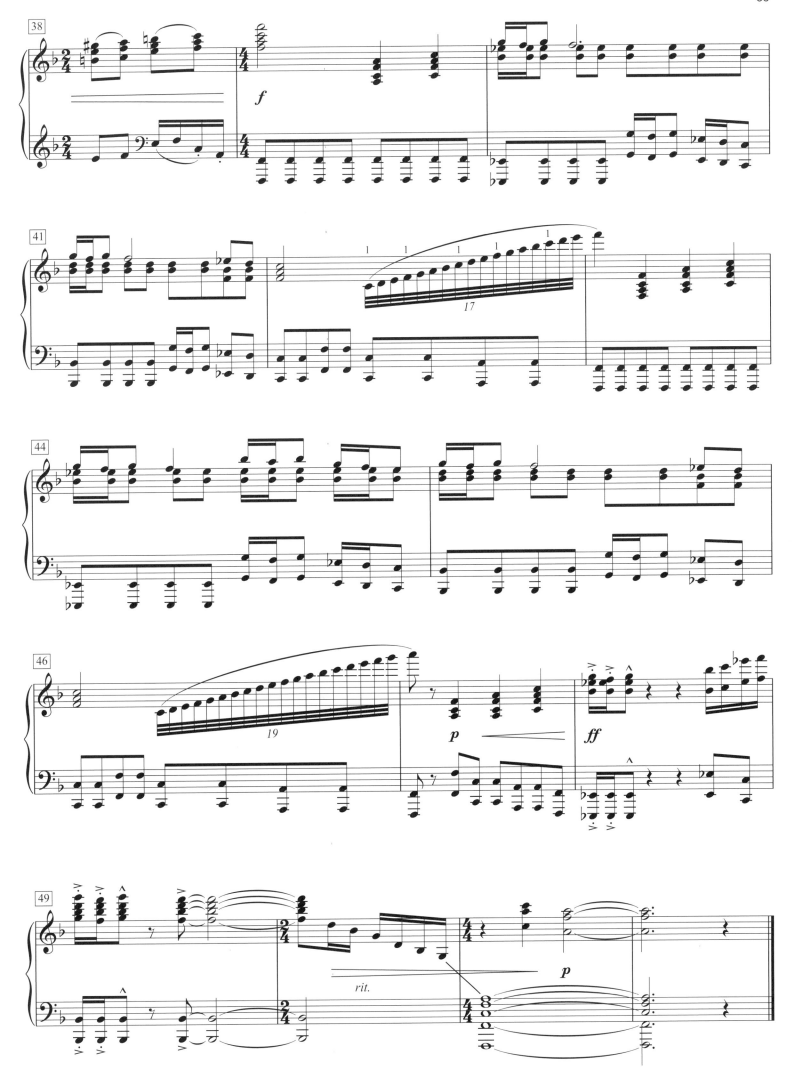

# LEAN ON ME

Words and Music by BILL WITHERS
Arranged by Phillip Keveren

Soulfully ♩ = 76

Copyright © 1972 INTERIOR MUSIC CORP.
Copyright Renewed
This arrangement Copyright © 2022 INTERIOR MUSIC CORP.
All Rights Controlled and Administered by SONGS OF UNIVERSAL, INC.
All Rights Reserved   Used by Permission

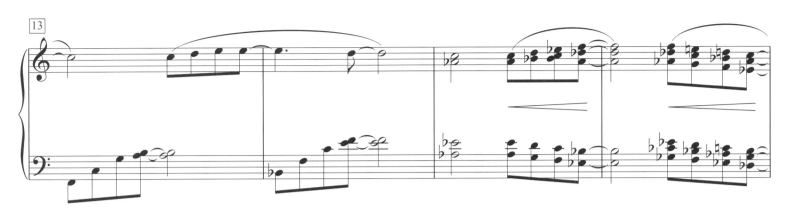

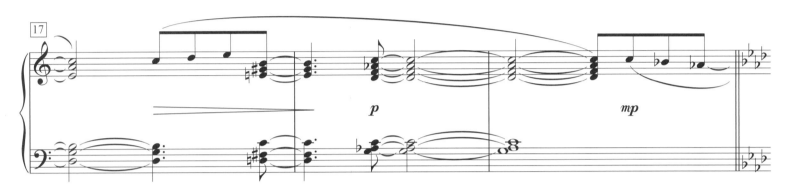

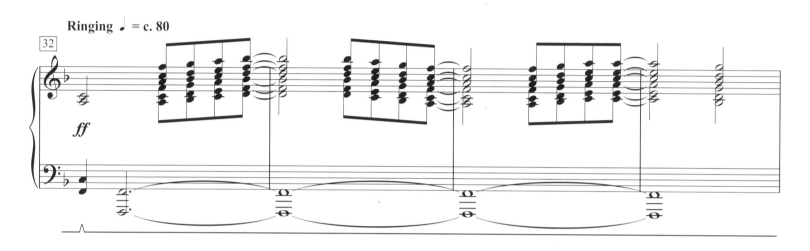

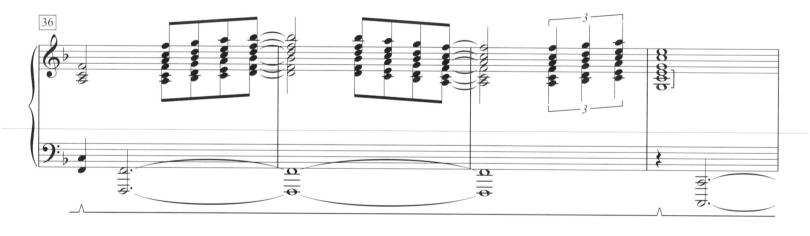

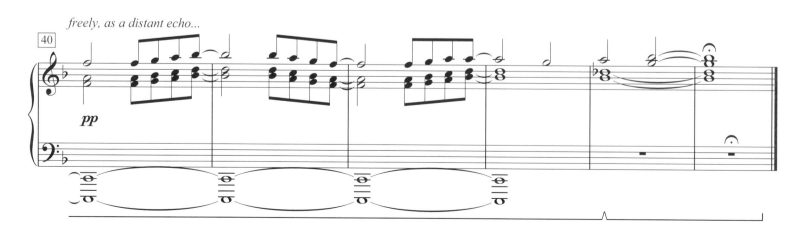

# PERFECT

Words and Music by ED SHEERAN
Arranged by Phillip Keveren

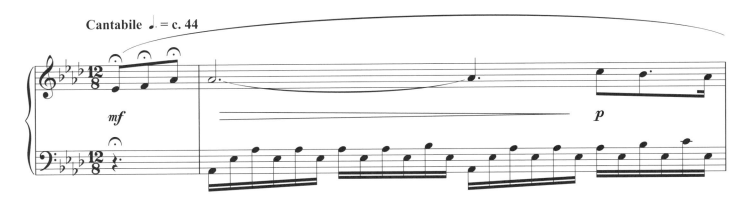

Copyright © 2017 Sony Music Publishing (UK) Limited
This arrangement Copyright © 2022 Sony Music Publishing (UK) Limited
All Rights Administered by Sony Music Publishing LLC, 424 Church Street, Suite 1200, Nashville, TN 37219
International Copyright Secured   All Rights Reserved

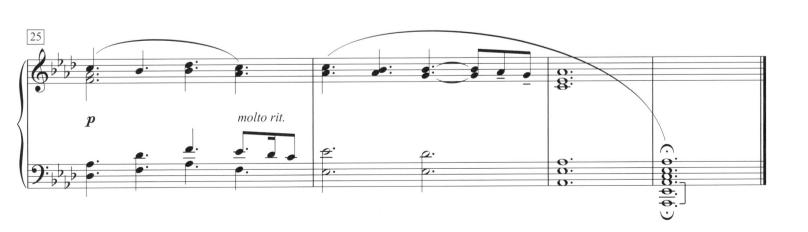

# OVER THE RAINBOW

Music by HAROLD ARLEN
Lyric by E.Y. "YIP" HARBURG
Arranged by Phillip Keveren

© 1938 (Renewed) METRO-GOLDWYN-MAYER INC.
© 1939 (Renewed) EMI FEIST CATALOG INC.
This arrangement © 2022 EMI FEIST CATALOG INC.
All Rights Administered by EMI FEIST CATALOG INC. (Publishing) and ALFRED MUSIC (Print)
All Rights Reserved   Used by Permission

# SIR DUKE

Words and Music by STEVIE WONDER
Arranged by Phillip Keveren

With a deep groove ♩ = 104

Copyright © 1976 Jobete Music Co., Inc. and Black Bull Music
Copyright Renewed
This arrangement Copyright © 2022 Jobete Music Co., Inc. and Black Bull Music
All Rights Administered by Sony Music Publishing LLC, 424 Church Street, Suite 1200, Nashville, TN 37219
International Copyright Secured   All Rights Reserved

# SO LONG, FAREWELL

### from THE SOUND OF MUSIC

Lyrics by OSCAR HAMMERSTEIN II
Music by RICHARD RODGERS
Arranged by Phillip Keveren

**Steady "tick-tock"** ♩ = 116

*With pedal*

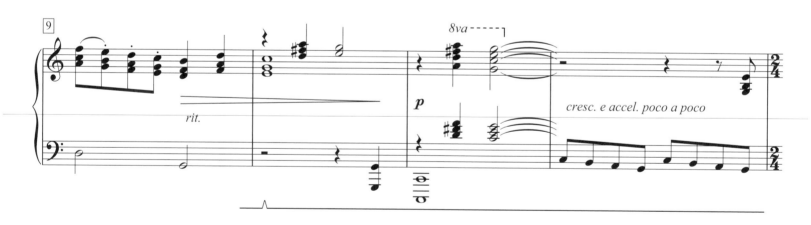

Copyright © 1959 Williamson Music Company c/o Concord Music Publishing
Copyright Renewed
This arrangement Copyright © 2022 Williamson Music Company c/o Concord Music Publishing
All Rights Reserved   Used by Permission

# SWEET CAROLINE

Words and Music by NEIL DIAMOND
Arranged by Phillip Keveren

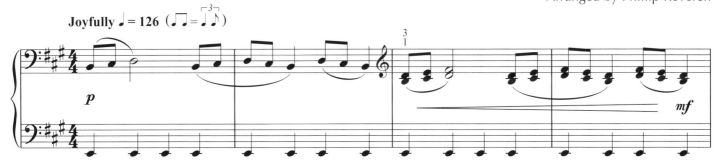

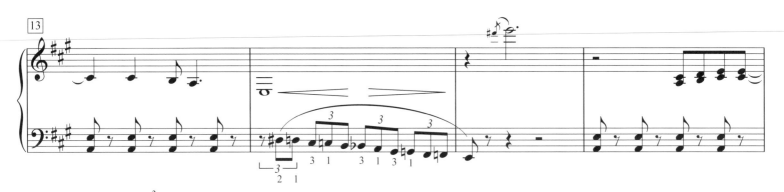

Copyright © 1969 STONEBRIDGE-MUSIC, INC.
Copyright Renewed
This arrangement Copyright © 2022 STONEBRIDGE-MUSIC, INC.
All Rights Administered by UNIVERSAL TUNES
All Rights Reserved   Used by Permission

# WATERMELON SUGAR

Words and Music by HARRY STYLES,
THOMAS HULL, MITCHELL ROWLAND
and TYLER JOHNSON
Arranged by Phillip Keveren

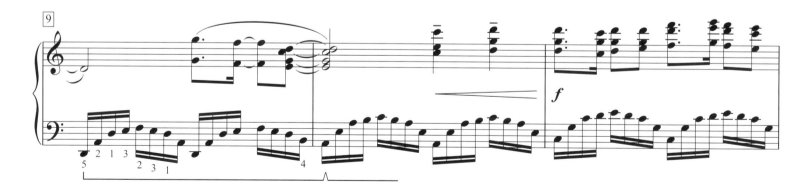

Copyright © 2019 HSA PUBLISHING LTD., UNIVERSAL MUSIC PUBLISHING LTD., SONGS OF UNIVERSAL, INC., SONGS BY CABIN MOBILE,
THESE ARE PULSE SONGS, ONE YEAR YESTERDAY PUBLISHING and CREATIVE PULSE MUSIC
This arrangement Copyright © 2022 HSA PUBLISHING LTD., UNIVERSAL MUSIC PUBLISHING LTD., SONGS OF UNIVERSAL, INC., SONGS BY CABIN MOBILE, THESE ARE PULSE SONGS,
ONE YEAR YESTERDAY PUBLISHING and CREATIVE PULSE MUSIC
All Rights for HSA PUBLISHING LTD. Administered by UNIVERSAL MUSIC WORKS
All Rights for UNIVERSAL MUSIC PUBLISHING LTD. Administered by UNIVERSAL - POLYGRAM INTERNATIONAL PUBLISHING, INC.
All Rights for SONGS BY CABIN MOBILE Administered by SONGS OF UNIVERSAL, INC.
All Rights for THESE ARE PULSE SONGS, ONE YEAR YESTERDAY PUBLISHING and CREATIVE PULSE MUSIC Administered by CONCORD COPYRIGHTS c/o CONCORD MUSIC PUBLISHING
All Rights Reserved   Used by Permission

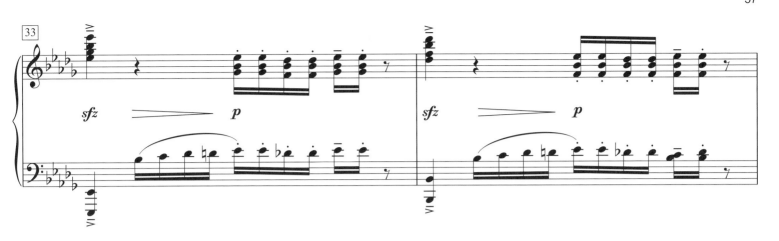

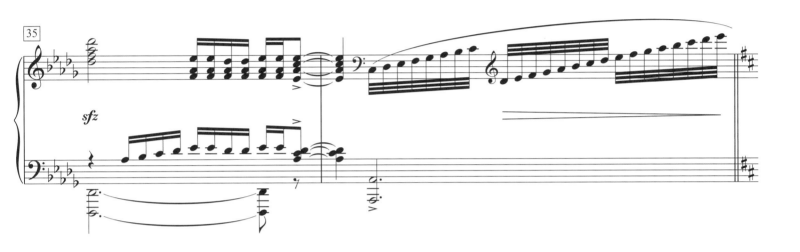

# WHEN I FALL IN LOVE

### from ONE MINUTE TO ZERO

Words by EDWARD HEYMAN
Music by VICTOR YOUNG
Arranged by Phillip Keveren

**Take your time - rubato...**

© 1952 (Renewed) CHAPPELL & CO., INC. and INTERSONG-USA, INC.
This arrangement © 2022 CHAPPELL & CO., INC. and INTERSONG-USA, INC.
All Rights Reserved   Used by Permission

# MORE EXCITING PIANO SOLOS
## by Phillip Keveren

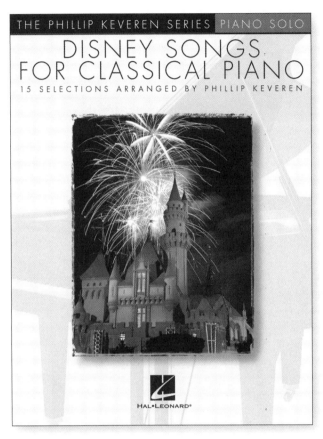

**HL 311754** DISNEY SONGS FOR CLASSICAL PIANO

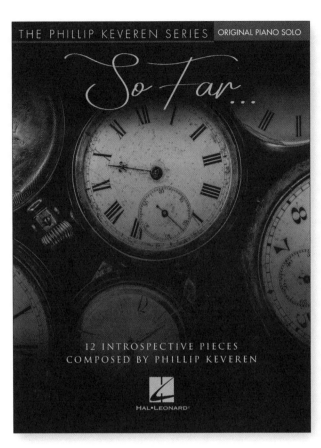

**HL 366023** SO FAR...

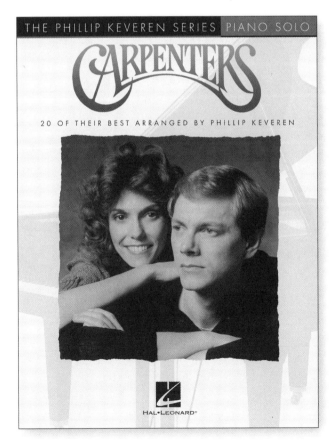

**HL 280848** CARPENTERS

**HL 198473** BACH MEETS JAZZ

# POPULAR SONGS
## HAL LEONARD STUDENT PIANO LIBRARY

The **Hal Leonard Student Piano Library** has great songs, and you will find all your favorites here: Disney classics, Broadway and movie favorites, and today's top hits. These graded collections are skillfully and imaginatively arranged for students and pianists at every level, from elementary solos with teacher accompaniments to sophisticated piano solos for the advancing pianist.

**Adele**
arr. Mona Rejino
Correlates with HLSPL Level 5
00159590..............................$12.99

**The Beatles**
arr. Eugénie Rocherolle
Correlates with HLSPL Level 5
00296649.............................. $12.99

**Irving Berlin Piano Duos**
arr. Don Heitler and Jim Lyke
Correlates with HLSPL Level 5
00296838..............................$14.99

**Broadway Favorites**
arr. Phillip Keveren
Correlates with HLSPL Level 4
00279192..............................$12.99

**Chart Hits**
arr. Mona Rejino
Correlates with HLSPL Level 5
00296710..............................$8.99

**Christmas at the Piano**
arr. Lynda Lybeck-Robinson
Correlates with HLSPL Level 4
00298194..............................$12.99

**Christmas Cheer**
arr. Phillip Keveren
Correlates with HLSPL Level 4
00296616..............................$8.99

**Classic Christmas Favorites**
arr. Jennifer & Mike Watts
Correlates with HLSPL Level 5
00129582..............................$9.99

**Christmas Time Is Here**
arr. Eugénie Rocherolle
Correlates with HLSPL Level 5
00296614..............................$8.99

**Classic Joplin Rags**
arr. Fred Kern
Correlates with HLSPL Level 5
00296743..............................$9.99

**Classical Pop – Lady Gaga Fugue & Other Pop Hits**
arr. Giovanni Dettori
Correlates with HLSPL Level 5
00296921..............................$12.99

**Contemporary Movie Hits**
arr. by Carol Klose, Jennifer Linn and Wendy Stevens
Correlates with HLSPL Level 5
00296780..............................$8.99

**Contemporary Pop Hits**
arr. Wendy Stevens
Correlates with HLSPL Level 3
00296836..............................$8.99

**Cool Pop**
arr. Mona Rejino
Correlates with HLSPL Level 5
00360103..............................$12.99

**Country Favorites**
arr. Mona Rejino
Correlates with HLSPL Level 5
00296861..............................$9.99

**Disney Favorites**
arr. Phillip Keveren
Correlates with HLSPL Levels 3/4
00296647..............................$10.99

**Disney Film Favorites**
arr. Mona Rejino
Correlates with HLSPL Level 5
00296809 ..............................$10.99

**Disney Piano Duets**
arr. Jennifer & Mike Watts
Correlates with HLSPL Level 5
00113759..............................$13.99

**Double Agent! Piano Duets**
arr. Jeremy Siskind
Correlates with HLSPL Level 5
00121595..............................$12.99

**Easy Christmas Duets**
arr. Mona Rejino & Phillip Keveren
Correlates with HLSPL Levels 3/4
00237139..............................$9.99

**Easy Disney Duets**
arr. Jennifer and Mike Watts
Correlates with HLSPL Level 4
00243727..............................$12.99

**Four Hands on Broadway**
arr. Fred Kern
Correlates with HLSPL Level 5
00146177..............................$12.99

**Frozen Piano Duets**
arr. Mona Rejino
Correlates with HLSPL Levels 3/4
00144294..............................$12.99

**Hip-Hop for Piano Solo**
arr. Logan Evan Thomas
Correlates with HLSPL Level 5
00360950..............................$12.99

**Jazz Hits for Piano Duet**
arr. Jeremy Siskind
Correlates with HLSPL Level 5
00143248..............................$12.99

**Elton John**
arr. Carol Klose
Correlates with HLSPL Level 5
00296721..............................$10.99

**Joplin Ragtime Duets**
arr. Fred Kern
Correlates with HLSPL Level 5
00296771..............................$8.99

**Movie Blockbusters**
arr. Mona Rejino
Correlates with HLSPL Level 5
00232850..............................$10.99

**The Nutcracker Suite**
arr. Lynda Lybeck-Robinson
Correlates with HLSPL Levels 3/4
00147906..............................$8.99

**Pop Hits for Piano Duet**
arr. Jeremy Siskind
Correlates with HLSPL Level 5
00224734..............................$12.99

**Sing to the King**
arr. Phillip Keveren
Correlates with HLSPL Level 5
00296808..............................$8.99

**Smash Hits**
arr. Mona Rejino
Correlates with HLSPL Level 5
00284841..............................$10.99

**Spooky Halloween Tunes**
arr. Fred Kern
Correlates with HLSPL Levels 3/4
00121550..............................$9.99

**Today's Hits**
arr. Mona Rejino
Correlates with HLSPL Level 5
00296646..............................$9.99

**Top Hits**
arr. Jennifer and Mike Watts
Correlates with HLSPL Level 5
00296894..............................$10.99

**Top Piano Ballads**
arr. Jennifer Watts
Correlates with HLSPL Level 5
00197926..............................$10.99

**Video Game Hits**
arr. Mona Rejino
Correlates with HLSPL Level 4
00300310..............................$12.99

**You Raise Me Up**
arr. Deborah Brady
Correlates with HLSPL Level 2/3
00296576..............................$7.95

7777 W. BLUEMOUND RD. P.O. BOX 13819 MILWAUKEE, WI 53213

Visit our website at **www.halleonard.com**

Prices, contents and availability subject to change without notice. Prices may vary outside the U.S.

# THE PHILLIP KEVEREN SERIES

## HAL•LEONARD®

Search songlists, more products and place your order from your favorite music retailer at **halleonard.com**

Disney characters and artwork
TM & © 2021 Disney LLC

## PIANO SOLO

*Prices, contents, and availability subject to change without notice.*